The Maccab[ees]
Tell The Story
Of Hanukkah

We're working on an app! Join us now & get it for free when we launch.

Unlimited illustrated children's stories like this one that teach **your** values (history, religion, family, courage, kindness, and much more) in one app including animations, music, read aloud, and even an option to insert familiar family faces into the story!

Welcome, friend!
I am Judas Maccabeus, and I am here to tell you about my family, and how they resisted against a whole empire.

Why does this story matter, you might ask? Well, I will let you know. By the end, you might recognize a certain holiday that is still celebrated right to this very day...

First, let me introduce my family. There are my brothers, John, Simon, Eleazar and Jonathan. We are known as the Maccabees (we will come to this name later). Everything began with our father, so perhaps he could begin the story for us?

'Thank you, my son. The story begins in a city near Jerusalem named Modein where I was a Kohen (Jewish priest). You see, there was an oppressive king named Antiochus who ruled over the empire at that time.'

'Antiochus believed everybody, including the Jews, should act like the Greeks. Including believing in the Greek gods, but we believe there is only one true God.'

'We were forbidden from reading the Law of Moses, and he burned any copies of it that he found. Not only that, but he banned us from observing the Sabbath and traditional feasts. Sacrifices of unclean animals were made in the temple.'

'He did all this because he could not tolerate people living differently to everyone else. We were forced to stop practicing our religion altogether.'

'Finally, he invaded and captured the holy city of Jerusalem. He insulted us by entering the Holy of Holies, the most sacred part of the Temple of Jerusalem where only the high priest is allowed. They ruined the oil that was used to light the menorah, the holy candles.'

'One day, I saw a fellow Jew on his way to make a sacrifice to the new Greek gods. I could take it no longer, and I struck the man, then fought with the king's soldier who was standing idly.'

People saw our father's example, and they too decided that enough was enough. They weren't going to stand by while the king turned us all into Greeks against our wishes. It wasn't fair. We needed to stand up and fight.

'My brother, let me tell the story of our fight!'
Of course, Johnathan. As the one who became my
successor, I could think of no better person.

'Now, Antiochus wasn't happy about anybody fighting back, so we had to escape into the hills. Our father was a priest, but we would become soldiers. From there, we brothers planned our rebellion..."

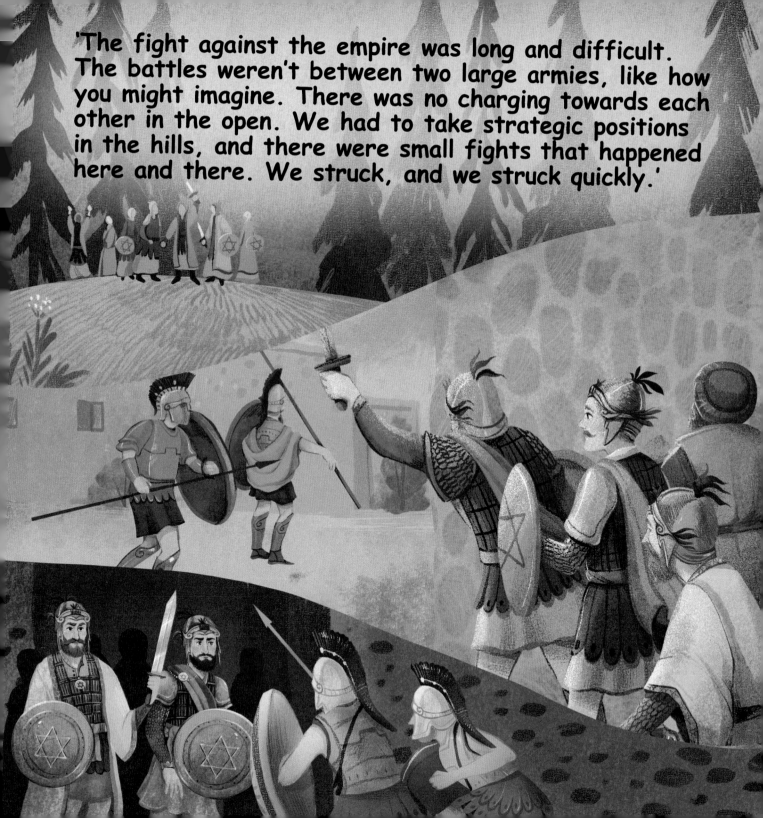

'The fight against the empire was long and difficult. The battles weren't between two large armies, like how you might imagine. There was no charging towards each other in the open. We had to take strategic positions in the hills, and there were small fights that happened here and there. We struck, and we struck quickly.'

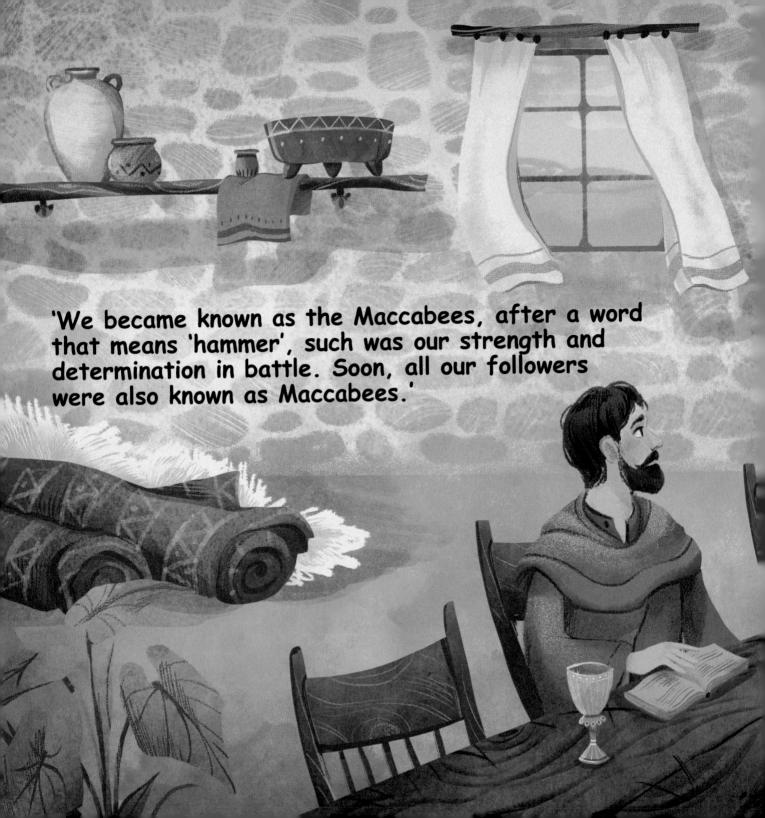

'We became known as the Maccabees, after a word that means 'hammer', such was our strength and determination in battle. Soon, all our followers were also known as Maccabees.'

Now brother, although the Maccabees fought very bravely, let's mention that we never forgot about our faith. I always made sure that we paused the fighting, so that our men could gather. 'We must remember to watch and pray,' I said.

We would read the Torah together. 'Remember how our fathers were saved at the Red Sea,' he told his men, speaking of Moses and Joshua, 'when Pharaoh with his forces pursued them'.

And then, just like in the days of Joshua, we blew our trumpets and were ready to fight the enemy once again with fresh enthusiasm.

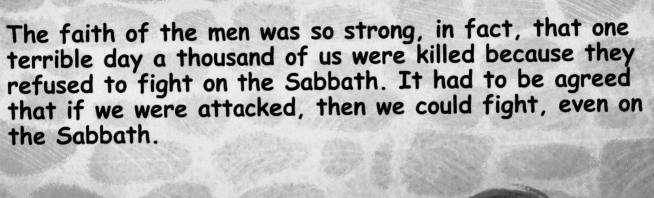

The faith of the men was so strong, in fact, that one terrible day a thousand of us were killed because they refused to fight on the Sabbath. It had to be agreed that if we were attacked, then we could fight, even on the Sabbath.

'Well said, brother. Perhaps I might tell the next part, about how we still celebrate these events?' Please do, Eleazar.

'So, after two years under the brave leadership of Judas, the Maccabees finally drove Antiochus's men out of Jerusalem. The first thing to do was to reclaim the temple after it had been ruined.'

'There was only enough oil to light the menorah for one day – the king's men had ruined the rest. So, they lit the menorah, expecting it to burn for one day and go out.'

'And that's when a miracle happened. The flames of the menorah's candle burned for eight whole nights, leaving the Maccabees time to find a fresh supply. This was the very first Hannukah, which means 'dedication."

So, every year from then on, there would be eight days of feasting and celebration. This is why the menorah now has eight branches. Every time we celebrate, we remember hope and togetherness.

And these things will always be important, even in these very different times.

Made in the USA
Coppell, TX
03 December 2024

41679185R00017